Nature Speaks

Mary Rosenbaum

PALMETTO
PUBLISHING

Charleston, SC
www.PalmettoPublishing.com

Nature Speaks
Copyright © 2023 by Mary Rosenbaum

Paperback ISBN: 979-8-8229-2585-4

A Day in The Woods

The yellow wings ascend without effort, almost playful
Taking the butterfly up, up, and over the top of the tall pine tree
Then down until lost in the midst of the forest.

The leaves of the short, young tree flutter in the wind
But make no sound
Yet I hear the music that it plays.

The buzzing begins slowly, and then the sound of all the insects
Crescendo to a loud chorus. As one begins, another ends.
Then there is silence.

I seek to hear the sounds only heard when listening.
All of Your creation sings.

Do I hear Your voice in the quietness? Is that the warmth and strength of Your arms as the sun penetrates through the crisp, fall air? When I see the richness of green around me, are You reminding me of life, rich and full? When the bird flits from one tree to another, are You telling me that You are a place of rest?

I long to hear Your every word to me, Your comfort sweet, and Your underserved mercy. Your creation is a gift of hope, of love, of faith - to me, at this moment, in Your presence.

I Am Yours

Blow Your wind
Upon my face
Help me sense
A taste of grace
I long to feel
Your firm embrace

I am Yours

You are here for me today
To show Your love
Come what may
Your work in me
Will never end
Only stay

I am Yours

May You lift
The veil for me
Just a glimpse
Is all I need
To see Your hand
Guiding me

I am Yours

From here to You
Is not so far
As raindrops fall
Upon my heart
The light shines through
 I see You

I am Yours

Awake

I awake to Your creation.
I breathe the spirit of Your presence.
As the white clouds hang in the blue sky,
As I walk amidst the tall trees,
I sense the greatness of Your power.
It causes me to fall to my knees.
As I touch the dirt,
As I feel the pebbles on my fingertips,
I am humbled.
Oh, the majesty of Your love!
Oh, the wonder of Your grace!
The song of my heart
Has found a resting place.

A New Season

A new season of change
Of hope
Of life
Comes slowly
Drifting in the wind
Like a leaf
Falling from a tree

The colors are vibrant
As the light of the sun
Follows its rocking motion
To the ground

There it will rest in stillness
Refreshed by the air of autumn

Its beauty for a time
Is appreciated from those
Who pass by

As time goes on
The colors fade
The leaf is melded with others
As it nurtures the earth from whence it came

Victory Sails

God loves me
I know it's true
He sent His Son
For me and you.
Some don't believe
They seek another way
A way without hope
Without forgiveness
Without love
God's love is so full
So great
God is love
His love washes over me
Through the moments.

Through the years
He was always near
For all my fears
With that cry
With that stumble
When I thought all
Would crumble
He held my hand
We walked

I did not always
Understand
His plan
I was pressed on the floor
No, no more
I stayed there a while
He picked me up
He helped me to stand
My feet were shaking
In the sifting sand
The waves came
Again and again
One was so deep
I wanted to sleep
The storm
The thunder
Could pull me under
Were it not for
His still small voice
Within
His love unfathomable
It was then
It was when
Victory sailed
Above the sea
No matter
All that was beneath

To Stand

The wind is depressing
As tree branches bend
From the forces of nature.
That which was strong and solid
In a moment begins to waver.
What do I know?
How can I stand?
The trembling of my soul
Courses through my body
Shaking me outwardly.
It could take me
Somewhere
Far away.
But then, I stand
On that I know to be true.
O God, it is You.

Open Praise

I thank You for the trees so tall
 Makes my cares seem so, so small
I thank You for the blue, blue sky
 The clouds that float right on by
I thank You for the birds that sing
 Their song such a wondrous thing

You meet my every single need
 You are the One who fills my dreams
Now I sing You open praise
 For all the world to see Your grace
It's found within the deepest place
 Your amazing grace!
How I long to see Your face
 Offer praise face to face

I thank You for the stars that shine
 Brilliant in the dark, dark night
You are there when all is lost
 To light the way by Your cross
My open praise I offer You
 In everything I say and do.

Reach Beyond

Reach beyond your grasp
To the great unknown
Step by step
Thought by thought
You can find much more
Than ever dreamed

There are some risks
Some hills to climb
With His loving hand to guide
Treasures are found
Stones of remembrance are placed
Our feet find solid ground

Mercy is needed
Grace is sufficient
Love touches us
As we draw near
His face is clear
He welcomes us home
Never more to roam
We sing His praise
In that heavenly place

The Mountain

As I walk up the mountain
I am consumed with getting to the top.
The steps require effort.
I notice others that have taken this path -
Wild ones who have learned to survive,
To carry on the balance of life in these woods.
I breathe deeply and enjoy knowing
Good oxygen is being pumped forcefully
Through my body as my heart beats faster.
Should I stop a moment or just press on?
I see some trees that have fallen in my path,
Some bushes I need to go around.
Finally, I reach my turning point.
It is marked well by boulders
That would seem to say, "Turn here."
I turn and begin walking another path
Down into the valley,
Back to the comforts of home.
The path is easy, though rather steep.
I need to notice where I step.

I see the pine needles gently move
As they are lifted by a breath of air.
I see the signs of spring -
Some deep purple leaves making an appearance,

A beautiful yellow bush close by,
A crimson red peeking through the trees.
I hear the sounds of birds singing,
Each singing their own song.
It is beautiful.
I am refreshed.
I add my song to theirs.
I am strengthened to climb the next mountain,
Climb a little higher.
I am steady. My help has come.

Psalm 121:1-2 "I will lift up mine eyes unto the hills from whence cometh my help. My help cometh from the Lord, which made heaven and earth." (KJV)

I AM

How can these things keep coming so hard and so fast?
I cry out to You in my time of need.
Put my feet on a mountain where I can see
Beyond the pain and turmoil
Of unsettled thoughts that rise within.
You are my fortress.
Will You be strong where I am weak?
Will You lift up when I am down?
Will Your promises hold
Even when the walls are crumbling,
The tears are flowing, and
My knees are on the ground?
Then I hear Your whispered voice,
"Be still and know that I am God.
I AM That I AM."

The Thread

The rain is falling.
My tear drops stopped.
The thoughts of my heart have not been wrought.
They are deeper still than man can tell.
But there is One who knows them well.
He finds the thread that runs so true,
The thread that binds the deep and what man can see.
He anchors my soul in the waters that flow and
Helps me stand still, unharmed and strong.

A Quiet Place

When the winds blow and the waves roar, there is a place of quiet in the midst of the storm. You are the peace that floods my soul. You are the strength that lets me stand.

As I Live

Lord, I love to call Your name.
It brings promise.
It gives hope.
Jesus.
It makes me smile
Knowing that You are there,
That You are here within me
Strong, secure, bright
Faithfully healing me
Constantly loving me
Giving me treasures
To hold close to my heart,
Guiding me on the path of light.
I'm leaning into Your presence,
Rejoicing in the shelter of Your wings.
I will take flight someday.
Let it not be only then, Lord.
May I now sail the seas and
Walk the promised land.
May my spirit soar to realms above
As I live, refreshed in praise to You.

This Day

When the sun's rays sift through the window
Your grace has reached me yet another day.
I walk the trail up the mountain.
The only sound I hear in the quietness
Is the crackling of twigs and leaves beneath my feet.
Oh, Your creation is glorious!
Upon my return, I enter another quiet place
Seeking Your heart, Your wisdom.
I read Your Word and pray what is prompted
By Your Holy Spirit.
The day continues with its joys,
With its challenges.
You are always there to guide,
To nourish,
To comfort.
Your strength and love
Make every day worth living.
To experience Your work in my life,
To know of Your work in the lives of others
Puts a smile on my face, and
Makes me know of Your presence.
Your touch makes all the difference.
As the day comes to a close
I remember the stretch of time in this day.
I bow my head in thankfulness.

Through The Years

God is able

When I am not.

His power goes on

When mine is lost.

I know He will carry me through.

There is nothing He cannot do.

When storms are rough

He brings the calm.

I fall on my knees.

He helps me see

There is a way after all.

All I need to do is humbly call.

His light will shine much more than mine.

Of that I'm sure

As the years go by.

My All in All

As I walk into this valley,
I know that You are by my side.
I don't know the path we'll follow,
But You will always be my guide.

The path sometimes is rocky.
It's cluttered by debris.
The clouds are all around me
So I can hardly see.

O Father, I will follow the path
That You will lead.
I may not climb a mountain or
Swim a rushing, mighty stream.
But I know that You will be there
To supply my every need.

You are my strength and shelter,
My rock, my staff, my call.
Where You lead me I will follow.
You are my all in all.

To Be Free

The hushed tweets of the birds
Capture my attention.
I strain to hear
A continuous melody of music.
It is not forth coming.

The wind blows.
The leaves
Flitter and flutter
As the branches sway
Back and forth,
Back and forth.

Sound is swept away
In a moment
As the dimming sky
Moves closer to the horizon.

I love the sound of silence,
The expectation of things to come
Born in my mind
No longer distracted
By things I see and hear.

My heart is playful
As it considers possibilities -
All the "what ifs."

A sense of victory
Of triumph
Holds me steadfast
As I let You rein me in
Put me on the path
I must follow
I must walk
To have peace
Flow like a river
Joy abound
As the waters
Gush with life
Hope serene always waiting
Always expecting
Knowing truth
Sets me free

Peace

The peace that comes from knowing You
Is deeper than the ocean
Further than my eye can see
Stronger than the tallest mountain
Closer than my heart strings

It is beyond my understanding
Lifts my soul to heights I cannot reach
It takes me one step further
Along this journey no man can see

Oh, what a wonderful companion
When life shatters hope and dreams
When words and thoughts might
Pull me under
Your peace makes a place for my feet

Halls

I hear cries of family and friends as they walk halls of pain, sorrow, and rejection. My own heart cries. Then the still small voice of hope is heard. A fountain of grace flows in the midst of His mercy.

Your Voice I Hear

What confidence
To belong to You
Your voice is near
That I might hear
And walk in Your ways
Obey
Serve
You only
Everywhere

In places where buildings are tall
The cement hard upon my feet
People coming and going
With no time to meet

In places of silence
Lofty mountains
Gently rolling meadows
Winding streams
Trees that touch the sky
Your blessings overtake me
You bring good
To everything that concerns me
My enemies run before me

Your holy promise
Forever mine
Your good treasure
Open before my eyes
Rejoicing
You give
Give
Give
Your word ever before me
That all may see and receive

The Great I Am

You are the lifter of my head
My almighty King
You are my tower of strength
My present help in trouble
You are my ever ready light
In the darkness
My blind eyes no longer see

You are the place where I lay my head
What a sweet, sweet bed!
Your loving arms enfold me
Bring me sleep
I awake with the freshness
Of a new morning
Painted by Your hand

I walk among the lilies
Yours is the Kingdom
The Power
The Glory
The Kingdom
In which I walk
In which I live
You are the Great I AM

Two Thoughts

I am alone.
The dark branches make it hard
To see the light.
The waves are crashing.
I am swallowed.
The well beneath me has strength
To pull me down, down, down.
There is crying in the air -
Lost hopes and broken dreams.
I sway back and forth,
Round and round.
Silence.
Will it break the sound?
Will I go deeper still?
Flowers and grass and children
A baby soft and quiet in the basket
Will its softness calm my soul?

I will reach and touch.
It is brighter now.
The light is all around.
No dark, no pain
Just joy and peace
Two thoughts, side by side
Struggling in one heart

To hold to one is to deny the other.
The worth of one stands alone
Strong and clear, always there.

The Conqueror

The winds of despair beat heavy
Upon the darkness of my soul.
They reach deep within
Trying to pull out memories
That would crush me.
I will not listen.
I will let the strength of my Lord
Conquer the winds of nature.
I will cling to His promises,
To His joy, to His comfort.
He has shown me the path of life
I will walk in it.

Here

I remember the place.
I wasn't able to write down my thoughts.
They are etched on my heart.
It is a quiet place with a few others near.
My spot is alone.
Trees have fallen and are criss-crossed
To form just the right place to sit.
I can look out from the tender, drooping branches
That form a natural umbrella.
I can see the land beyond
Scattered with barns, fences, gardens,
Trees reaching to the sky.
My little spot is cozy.
The sun is shining hot outside.
Here I can feel
The refreshing cool of the shade.
Here I can stop for a minute and
Hear the sounds of nature but also
The meditation of my heart.
Here things fall into place.
Here life is more simple.
Here things that matter are made clear.
Here peace and hope stand side by side.
Here joy rings
Like the dawn of a new morning.

With You

With You I can go on.
My steps are strengthened.
My feet are steady.
I look beyond the things of this life,
The things that shield Your face
And pull me slowly, slowly
Until You reach for me in Your mercy.

Your love dispels the weight.
Your touch brings something new.
You call me to walk with You,
To be refreshed in Your goodness,
The flowers of the morning,
The sun of midday,
The stillness of night.
With You I have the hope of tomorrow,
Rest from the past, and
Joy for today.

The Coming Rain

Rain is in the forecast. Maybe, just maybe I can get up that mountain before the torrent comes. I start the climb with the overcast sky looming above. I hear the whistling, whining, warbling sounds of the birds as they orchestrate their own symphony. A few drops of water moisten my clothes. It is refreshing. My steps become more determined as I reach the top and start the downward stretch. The song of the birds seems muffled as the rain comes stronger but still softly. Then as the raindrops lessen, the chorus of birds is stronger once again. They have been refreshed as I. The moo of a black cow in the distance adds to the contentment of us all. God loves His creation. He prepares us for the torrential rain to come. He preserves life. He has a place and a purpose for all of His creation.

Through My Window

The rapid jittery, fluttering of the leaves near the top of the trees draw my attention. It is hard to miss these high notes of today's concert. They still are bright with the colors of the autumn season, but also cling as if it might be their last chance before falling to the cold ground beneath. Branches of the evergreen pine pipe in now and then as they sway softly in the wind making their own music low and steady like a bow skimming over a string. Behind the pines I see leaves of several trees moving with a rhythm of their own, filling in all that might be missing in this concert of life. Fallen needles and leaves of various colors have found a place of rest at the base of each tree. The carpet of green grass before me is beginning to fade but still vibrant with the life of an experienced conductor. A few shrubs here and there are already adorned with red berries, a bright symbol of coming winter snows. The crooked gray branches of the peach tree come into view. Right now it adds a woeful sound as if all is lost. Spring will come.

Come Now

I cry, I cry, I cry.
Struggle. Is there no end?
When needs and pain press heavily on my chest,
The deep pulls me down as if to whisper or maybe shout,
"You can't get out!"
How will I ever have the strength to rise above the pain,
The sadness, the deception?
Come now, Lord, and touch me strong.
I am weary.
When the pull is downward,
Lift me with Your steady, gentle hands.
May what is in the deep bring strength and joy
Unexplained, but strong and bright.
Make me to sing a new song,
A song of peace and understanding
That reaches beyond the deep,
To the brightness of the sun behind the clouds.

Walking The Trails

Though I did not find colorful flowers on those walking paths, I was blessed with green, green, and more green. From the green moss that edged the roads to the green ferns, bushes, and trees in their spring green, I was blessed. I noticed several trees that had fallen and were in varying states of decay. Winding vines and small limbs were twisted this way and that sometimes forming mathematical shapes – squares, triangles, ovals, circles, some partially formed. Some limbs didn't seem to know which way to grow – straight and strong reaching for the skies or bending over to the forces of nature. The swampy land area added a mysterious touch to the land with its small swampy knots like elongated doorknobs reaching up out of the wetlands. Spanish moss clung to a few chosen branches. I heard birds sing and squirrels chatter. A living green was almost everywhere. Nevertheless, brown crackling leaves still found their place on the forest floor. The woods and winding trails were a picture of life in many ways. May we have grateful hearts as we walk with Him through life.

Walk With Me

Your Words
I hear them
I think on them
What do they mean?
Are they for me?
How?

Could it really be
You see me
Unfettered and free
Confident with glee
Glad to be me
All You created me to be

Rise
Walk with Me
Believe
Never again be held back
No more

The words that despise
Mock
Push
Tear down

They trample
Hold you there

Let them go
Walk with Me
Believe

As we walk
Waters will part
Fire will be quenched
Your feet will be steady
On the edge of the mountain
In the deep cutting canyons

No way to pass?
No way to go on?
Time has you
In its clutch
Holds you tight

Time has no hold on
My Word
Its Truth
I am there
I lift you
I carry you
We go through

Together
Where you've never gone
Beyond your imagination
Your strength
Me alone
Your safety
All my own
Walk with Me
Believe